How to Increase Confidence and Succeed in Meeting People: Business Networking the Easy Way...Meet New People Now!

Calvin K. Lee, MBA, CPA, CA, CPA (Illinois)

ISBN-13: 978-1522777977
ISBN-10: 1522777970

I0489011

Praise from readers

"Good read. Networking is so important at work, church and even personal life. How can we take charge and embrace it? Very practical, good reading!"
- V.C.

"By using his own example, Calvin gives hope for the readers."
- J.L.

"Five stars. Great real life experience that you can relate to easily."
- D.L.

Table of Contents

Praise from readers

Table of Contents

1. Does networking make you scared?

2. Defining networking

3. Can introverts become good at networking?

4. The benefit of networking

5. Networking like a pro

6. You never know who knows who!

7. Maintaining your network

CONCLUSION

ABOUT THE AUTHOR

Contact the author

Other books by Calvin K. Lee

FREE book sample from:

"Living an Extraordinary and Amazingly Purposeful Life: 9 Principles to a Better Life"

FREE book sample from:

"Words of Wisdom, Encouragement, and Inspiration"

FREE book sample from:

"How to Work Smarter, Not Harder: Success in the Workplace"

FREE book sample from:

"A Collection of Short Stories"

FREE book sample from:

"Bookkeeping and Accounting Step-by-step Basics for Small & Medium sized Businesses and Home Businesses: Over 20 Examples of Common Accounting Transactions!"

FREE book sample from:

"Understanding Financial Statement Analysis

for Accountants, Business Owners, Investors, and Stakeholders"

FREE book sample from:

"LEAP before you THINK"

About the Author

Contact the author

Other books by Calvin K. Lee

1. Does networking make you scared?

Networking...

Did you shudder just hearing that word? Does networking give you the chills? Are you afraid of not knowing what to say and facing the awkward silence?

Fear not, my friend. I was once in your position. In fact, when I was in elementary school, I was so shy that one of my few friends said to me during an Andy Warhol art exhibit fieldtrip: "Calvin, you don't have any friends." Ouch. I still remember that day clearly. He said it while we were near the top of the escalator.

In high school, I wasn't very popular either. I always envied people who were naturally outgoing, serving on student council, having lots of friends, going to parties, etc. I wasn't invited to many parties.

In university I remember one day I was walking around thinking, why do I fear being around other people? Why do I have to keep wearing this mask of confidence? Why can't I just be myself? Why can't I naturally be like those outgoing people to whom talking and socializing (gulp) comes so easily?

Fast forward to today, I have grasped the basics of networking, and a lot of people ask me how I do networking so easily. One of my professors saw me networking with my classmates before class and said, "Calvin, you're a social butterfly!" I get invited to a lot of events, and am still having fun meeting new people.

This is a short book on how I went from dreading networking to embracing it. And with some effort, you can do it too. If I can do it, you can do it.

2. Defining networking

I define networking as meeting people you don't know with the purpose of making more friends, business contacts, and building professional networks.

Networking does not mean hanging out with the people you know all the time.

Networking isn't one of those things you can learn completely out of a book. It's like learning to ride a bicycle. Sure you'll be wobbly at first, but it's interesting that to maintain balance you can't stand still. You have to move and create momentum in order to stay balanced on a bicycle. It's the same with networking. You can't stand still and not go talk to someone. You have to get out of your comfort zone and just say, "Hi." You have to throw yourself out there and trust you will survive.

If I can do it, you can do it too.

I've met resistance from people when I tell them about the benefits of networking. They would argue that close friends and connections are enough. While having close friends are important, people who are not used to networking cannot understand the tremendous value of networking because they have never done it and have never seen the amazing results that come from networking.

People who like to stay in their own comfort zone with their close group of friends do not understand the power of "Weak ties". Weak ties are the people you see just occasionally in a year, maybe once or twice a year, and you don't see them on a regular basis. When it comes to finding a job, it is well documented by other authors and articles on LinkedIn that "Weak ties" have tremendous potential to helping you with your career. This is because your close group of friends likely has the same circle of people as you. This really limits the amount of people you and your close friends know. However, "Weak ties" are generally outside your close circle of friends and so the number of people they know can be quite significant.

3. Can introverts become good at networking?

I expect some readers of this book are introverts. You hate networking. Extroverts by nature get energized when they are around people, so they tend to naturally like networking (socializing).

There are differences between introverts and extroverts. If you are an introvert, you could only be successful for a while at pretending to be an extrovert before you run out of energy and need to rest for a few days. That's right – if you push yourself to be an extrovert, you may need to go hide and rest for days.

First, you need to know being shy and needing solitude are two completely separate things. If you're an introvert, that's not going to change. You still need your solitude times to regenerate your energy when you're alone. However, you can overcome your shyness and can get out there and meet people.

There are many famous introverts: Abraham Lincoln and Bill Gates are just two examples.

I believe introverts can grow into ambiverts. Ambiverts are people who can use characteristics from both introverts and extroverts. It's a matter of practice being brave. You can become an ambivert by practicing networking skills.

4. The benefit of networking

You probably already know the benefits of networking, or if you don't, a simple Google search would give you hundreds if not thousands of results. I will point out main benefit of networking that I find most useful myself.

Benefit: Networking is great for looking for a job.

People say most jobs are never advertised. The hiring manager will first ask his or her staff if they know anybody who can fill the position. Then the hiring manager may ask other departments to see if any internal candidates or people the staff know can fill the position. This all happens before the job is posted, and by this point, many jobs are already filled. That's why you want to network and try to get this inside information.

5. Networking like a pro

When I attend an event, I aim to start my networking at the top. Every event has limited time, and you have limited energy. You want the best bang for your buck. What I mean by starting at the top is to meet the organizers of an event. They will likely be wandering around the room with an officially looking nametag that is computer printed with a nice company logo, while the other participants are all wearing sticker nametags.

Why should you start with the organizers of an event? They can easily introduce you to other people. They will likely know a lot of people in the room, and they can introduce you to other members of the organizing committee. In other words, they are a great resource to start.

It's also easy to start a conversation with the organizers. You already know a lot about them. They organized the event. You can tell them they organized a great event, ask them how long it took to organize, how many guests are expected to come, etc.

Don't worry so much about your own performance. If you focus and enjoy what the other person is saying, it takes a lot of pressure of you. People love to talk about themselves. Once you learn how to get people to talk about themselves, just open both ears and listen!

6. You never know who knows who!

I network with everyone, with people above my level, people at the same level as me, and people below my level. Yes, even with people I consider below my level. The rationale is simple: you never know who knows who! That administrative assistant may just know a CEO or manager who's currently hiring. They have that information that you don't have! The point is you never know who knows who. That's why while you should focus on certain groups of people to network with, don't neglect to network with people who seem outside of your circle.

The more you network, the easier it becomes. The first time you go networking, you may not know anyone. As I'm writing this I attended a new networking event for me this morning that I only knew one person. By the end of the event, I knew nearly 20 people. Next time I come back to a similar event, I'll probably meet a few people I've met already today. As you can see, networking can be fun!

7. Maintaining your network

The longer it takes you to re-establish contact with a person the less useful that connection will be to you when you need to use your network. I recommend you contact important people in your network on at least an annual basis. It's simple if you use LinkedIn. LinkedIn has a feature in which it e-mails you when a connection has a work anniversary or a new job. That's the best time to send them an e-mail and say congratulations.

Here's a sample on how you can use an e-mail to congratulate a connection on their new job or work anniversary:

Hi Bob,

LinkedIn sent me a message that you're celebrating 8 years working at ABC Bank! Congratulations!

I've just celebrated 3 years working at XYZ Company myself this past April.

Best Regards,
Calvin

I usually try to mention something about how I'm doing so my contact has something to talk about. As well, it keeps them in the loop on how your career is doing.

If you enjoyed this book, please support me by leaving a positive review on Amazon. Click here to review. Alternatively, scroll to the end of this book and in the "Before you go" section, click on the stars and leave a review. As a bonus, after you leave a review, e-mail me at hellocalvinlee@gmail.com and I'll send you a FREE PDF version of this book. When I see a review, I am more encouraged to write more books.

Join my Facebook author fan page for new books:
https://www.facebook.com/hellocalvinlee/

CONCLUSION

Well, there you have it. I have given you many networking tips and advice I've learned by trial-and-error. Now all that's left to do is for you to get out there, and immerse yourself with networking. Start small, set a goal of talking to 1-2 people whom you don't know. If you're adventurous, start with 5 people like I did. The benefits are numerous. Most of all have fun. You'll enjoy the journey a lot more!

Happy networking!

I hope you've found this book useful and can keep it at your desk as a quick reference tool.

IMPORTANT! Scroll to the end of this book and in the "before you go" section, click the stars and leave a review. Alternatively, please go to Amazon's website and rate my book. It takes a minute to rate the number of stars and it will help other readers see that you enjoyed my book and so they can also benefit from it. Please also leave a comment on what you enjoyed most from the book. This will be really helpful for my books to attract more readers so more people can benefit. I appreciate your assistance!

Click here to go to my Amazon Author page: http://goo.gl/4UQfJW. You can also search Amazon for "Calvin K Lee" for my other books. You will find them inspirational and improve the quality of your life.

ABOUT THE AUTHOR

Calvin K. Lee, MBA, CPA, CA, CPA (Illinois) holds a MBA degree with distinction from York University in Toronto, Canada and is expecting a Double MBA degree from Peking University in Beijing, China in 2016. He is also a U.S. Certified Public Accountant, Canadian Chartered Professional Accountant, and Chartered Accountant. He has served as President of the MBA Ambassadors during his MBA studies and as Chair of the Young Professionals Forum at the CPA Association. He has lived in Beijing, Hong Kong, Toronto, and Vancouver.

Contact the author

Want a FREE PDF version of this book? Subscribe to my e-mail list by sending an e-mail with the book title as the subject line to hellocalvinlee@gmail.com. I will e-mail you a free PDF version of this book.

Facebook fan page: https://www.facebook.com/hellocalvinlee

E-mail: hellocalvinlee@gmail.com
Twitter: @calvinklee2010

If there are any topics you want me to write about in a future book, I'd love to know!
I welcome feedback and comments.

Other books by Calvin K. Lee

Click here to go to my Amazon author page with all my books. **Or click each link below for each book.**

1. How to Increase Confidence and Succeed in Meeting People: Business Networking the Easy Way: Meet New People Now!

2. Living an Extraordinary and Amazingly Purposeful Life: 9 Principles to a Better Life

3. Words of Wisdom, Encouragement, and Inspiration: Bring Happiness into Your Life

4. How to Work Smarter, Not Harder: Success in the Workplace

5. A Collection of Short Stories: And the Moral of the Story is...?

6. Bookkeeping and Accounting Step-by-step Basics for Small & Medium Sized Businesses and Home Businesses: Over 20 Examples of Common Accounting Transactions!

7. Understanding Financial Statements: For Accountants, Business Owners, Investors, and Stakeholders

8. LEAP before you THINK

FREE book sample from:

"Living an Extraordinary and Amazingly Purposeful Life: 9 Principles to a Better Life"

©2015 Calvin Lee
All rights reserved

Living an
Extraordinary
and Amazingly
Purposeful
Life

9 Principles to a
Better Life

Calvin K. Lee, MBA, CPA

Table of Contents

Introduction
1. How do I step out of my comfort zone?
2. What are you thinking?
3. Be yourself
4. Know yourself
5. Don't let other people run your life
6. Set a S.M.A.R.T. goal!
7. Take risks!
8. Who do you want as friends?
9. Continuous learning
Final thoughts
About the author
Other books by Calvin Lee

Note to the reader

This book is written for general guidance, and is not a substitute for accounting, legal, tax, or other professional advice with a qualified advisor. Laws are always changing. While every effort is made to make this book current, there may be errors or omissions. This book is made available with no representations or warranties of any kind for the accuracy or completeness of this book. The author and/or publisher do not assume and hereby disclaim any liability or responsibility for any action or decision leading to claims, losses or damages by any person(s) relying on the contents of this book. Consult a professional advisor as needed as the examples may or may not be applicable to your situation.

Praise from readers for Calvin's books:

"Very practical, good reading!"

"I really enjoy your books."

"Well done, very informative. I like how you used your example."

"By using his own example, Calvin gives hope for the readers."

"Great real life experience that you can relate to easily."

"Very clear, concise, and concrete. Well done."

"Practical tips and relatable examples. A pleasant read. Congratulations on your recent publications! Keep writing more."

"Thanks for the little pearls of wisdom and optimism."

Introduction

Most people want to live an extraordinary life, but not everybody who wants to does.

With effort, I believe everyone and everybody who wants to live an extraordinary life can. In my own life, I've lived in four different cities, met hundreds of people from all over the world, and enjoy a career that I love. I consider my life extraordinary even though I am just a very normal, average person growing up in a normal, average household. The key is the attitude of the mind, as well as taking appropriate action.

Turn the page and let the journey begin!

1. How do I step out of my comfort zone?

People love their comfort zone. That's why they don't live extraordinary lives.

First of all, you have to have a deep desire for a better life, and you'll do anything to get it. And that means some temporary discomfort. People get bored of routine. You work the same job every day, but you don't change. The most likely reason is the current job is comfortable.

What I've found in my own journey is the decision to step out is the most difficult part. I remember going to zip line some years ago, where there is a wire hanging between two high poles with the rider strapped into a harness and fly across the two poles at a very fast speed.

We were required to climb up a really tall pole, the height of an electric cable pole, two or three stories high. As someone who is afraid of heights, climbing up the pole was scary, I had to remind myself to not look down. But climbing wasn't the scariest part. I remember there was a small platform at the top to sit on, the moment before you jump. I was horrified, petrified, mortified. I remember thinking to myself, "What did I get myself into?" After a few seconds of hesitation, which felt like eternity, I leaped off the platform, and had the thrill of my life zip lining. Once I made the jump, I was no longer afraid.

KEY POINT: To live an extraordinary and amazing life...You have to jump and take a leap of faith!

What does this mean in real life?

Several years ago I remember joining a volunteer committee for my profession to organize educational & social events for young professionals. I was a committee member and one day, the chairperson announced she was stepping down, and asked for volunteers to take over her role. I was excited at the opportunity, but I also had my doubts. Fear and worries flooded my mind:

Who am I to take this role? Do I have what it takes?
I don't have the experience.
What if I don't do a good job?

Knowing that the longer I hesitate the more worries and excuses my mind will come up with, I decided to take a leap of faith and just raise my hand and volunteer. The rest is history.

PUT IT INTO PRACTICE: Try to step out of your comfort zone a little everyday. That way, when a big decision comes up, you'll be more ready to take the leap of faith.
Do this, and you're well on your way to an extraordinary life!

Click here now to get your copy: 2. Living an Extraordinary and Amazingly Purposeful Life: 9 Principles to a Better Life (Book #2)

FREE book sample from:

"Words of Wisdom, Encouragement, and Inspiration"

Table of Contents
Introduction
1. How to be successful
2. Be thankful
3. Words of encouragement in pain and suffering
4. A brighter day will surely come
5. Words of wisdom on love
6. You are unique!
7. Fake it till you make it!
8. More words of wisdom
Final thoughts
About the Author
Other books by Calvin K. Lee

Note to the reader

This book is written for general guidance, and is not a substitute for accounting, legal, tax, or other professional advice with a qualified advisor. Laws are always changing. While every effort is made to make this book current, there may be errors or omissions. This book is made available with no representations or warranties of any kind for the accuracy or completeness of this book. The author and/or publisher do not assume and hereby disclaim any liability or responsibility for any action or decision leading to claims, losses or damages by any person(s) relying on the contents of this book. Consult a professional advisor as needed as the examples may or may not be applicable to your situation.

Praise from readers for Calvin's books:

"Very practical, good reading!"

"I really enjoy your books."

"Well done, very informative. I like how you used your example."

"By using his own example, Calvin gives hope for the readers."

"Great real life experience that you can relate to easily."

"Very clear, concise, and concrete. Well done."

"Practical tips and relatable examples. A pleasant read. Congratulations on your recent publications! Keep writing more."

"Thanks for the little pearls of wisdom and optimism."

1. How to be successful

Thomas Edison took more than 1,000 attempts to invent the electric light bulb. Did he say he failed 1,000 times? No, he said he was successful in finding 1,000 ways *not* to make a light bulb.

With every rejection, you are one step closer to success.

You reap what you sow. What you don't sow is what you won't reap.

There is a fire of passion inside of you. All you have to do is find it and rekindle it.

All successful people have a clear purpose and goal.

Thinking is hard work, which is why so few people do it. Those who can think succeed.

Everyone has the potential to succeed. Frequently it's not a lack of skill that prevents people from success, but rather fear: fear of the unknown, fear of rejection, fear of success, fear of rejection, fear of being different. What do you fear?

It is said the journey of a thousand miles begins with a single step. Success does not come overnight, it comes through a series of steps. Sometimes it's two steps forward and one step back.

Don't despair. Every setback and rejection brings you one step closer to your goal.

You know you can do it. Believe in yourself!

If it is to be, why not me?

Successful people are always looking for opportunities to help others. Unsuccessful people are always asking, "What's in it for me?"

If you've never failed, it means you've never tried. If you've never tried things beyond your comfort zone, you've likely never failed.

Money spent can be re-earned, but experience is mine to keep for the rest of my life.

If you want to succeed, cut the following from your vocabulary: "I should have", "I could have", "I would have". Now take concrete action.

The difference between winners and ordinary people is winners follow through despite fear while others just dream and take no action.

Learning to delay instant gratification is crucial to success. A research study put a child in an empty room with a cookie in front of them. The researcher tells the child he will leave the room for a while. The child can choose to take the cookie, but if the child can wait until the researcher comes back, the researcher will give the child two cookies. The research showed children that can wait and delay instant gratification are more successful in life.

Click here now to get your copy on Amazon: 3. Words of Wisdom, Encouragement, and Inspiration: Bring Happiness into Your Life (Book #3)

FREE book sample from:

"How to Work Smarter, Not Harder: Success in the Workplace"

Table of Contents

About the Author

Introduction: smart ways to work

1. Techniques to instantly brighten up your day: smile and whistle

2. Working smarter: know if you're a morning person or a night owl

3. Change your attitude and approach

4. Exercise becomes more important as busyness increases

5. Improve your biggest asset: your mind

6. Meditation: it gives you a sense of more time

7. Improve your creativity by doing something relaxing

8. Know yourself: your personality, likes & dislikes, strengths & weaknesses

9. Avoid multitasking: finish one task before starting another

10. Improve attention span

Final Thoughts

Other Books by Calvin K. Lee

Note to the reader

This book is written for general guidance, and is not a substitute for accounting, legal, tax, or other professional advice with a qualified advisor. Laws are always changing. While every effort is made to make this book current, there may be errors or omissions. This book is made available with no representations or warranties of any kind for the accuracy or completeness of this book. The author and/or publisher do not assume and hereby disclaim any liability or responsibility for any action or decision leading to claims, losses or damages by any person(s) relying on the contents of this book. Consult a professional advisor as needed as the examples may or may not be applicable to your situation.

Introduction: smart ways to work

There are many ways to work, but some ways are smarter than other ways. For example, how many ways there are to get from San Francisco to New York City? Here are some options:

1. Walk there
2. Run there
3. Ride a bicycle there
4. Drive a car there
5. Take a plane there

All of these ways will get you from San Francisco to New York City...eventually. It's just that some ways are smarter than other ways. All of these ways eventually work, but some ways are smarter and more efficient than others. In today's day and age, time is of the essence. You've heard the saying, "Time is money."

KEY POINT: there are multiple ways to solve every problem, but some ways are smarter than other ways.

Some of the suggestions in this book can be implemented immediately and effortlessly, immediately improving your work life. Other suggestions take time to change an old habit to a new one. Be patient with yourself while trying to change. It takes effort but you will receive huge dividends later.

Kids are incredibly creative. If you ask them to stand in the corner and face the wall, they will find a fun way to spend the time there. They will invent a game with himself or herself, sing a song, wave their arms, or see how long they can hold their breath.

I love watching kids play at the park. They are incredibly creative in what they do. They don't need people to tell them how to play. They innately know how to have fun. Unfortunately, as we grow to be adults we lose that sense of creativity. We think there is one "right" way to do things, and we do it over and over again. Fortunately for us, we all have a kid living inside of us. We were once kids, with limitless imagination and energy. But our school system taught us to sit still, learn the 'right' way to do things, and just follow what others do.

KEY POINT: Each of us can let the creative child inside of us be imaginative and have fun. In the creative process, you'll find smarter ways to work!

We can tap into our imagination and find smarter ways to do things. Let the creative child inside of you blossom again. You'll experience life in a whole new way doing your routine tasks!

PUT IT INTO ACTION: For every task you do, try to find a smarter way to do it. Be creative and have some fun!

1. Techniques to instantly brighten up your day: smile and whistle

If you're in a happy mood, you work smarter than when you are in a grumpy mood. There are many simple ways to lift your mood and brighten up your day within minutes.

KEY POINT: You work smarter when you're in a good mood.

The first way is to smile, whether you feel like it or not. Once I was really stressed out at work. I had nothing to smile about, but I forced my face to smile. Doing that changes the chemistry in your body that actually makes you feel better. It's true when you feel a certain emotion, your body would physically mimic that emotion. For example, if you feel happy, your face would naturally smile. The reverse is also true. If you make your body physically do something, you will start feeling the accompanying emotion.

Another way to instantly brighten up your day is to whistle, or hum a song. It's hard to whistle and feel grumpy at the same time. You've probably heard the song lyrics that go, "whistle while you work." It will make you happier instantly. Then you can work smarter.

PUT IT INTO ACTION: smile even if you don't feel like it. Whistle if your work place allows it, or hum quietly to yourself. All of these simple yet powerful techniques can lift your mood within a short period of time and significantly improve the quality of your work. You can also try other actions like snapping your fingers or clapping your hands.

Click here now to get your copy from Amazon: 4. How to Work Smarter, Not Harder: Success in the Workplace (Book #4)

FREE book sample from:

"A Collection of Short Stories"

©2015 Calvin Lee
All rights reserved

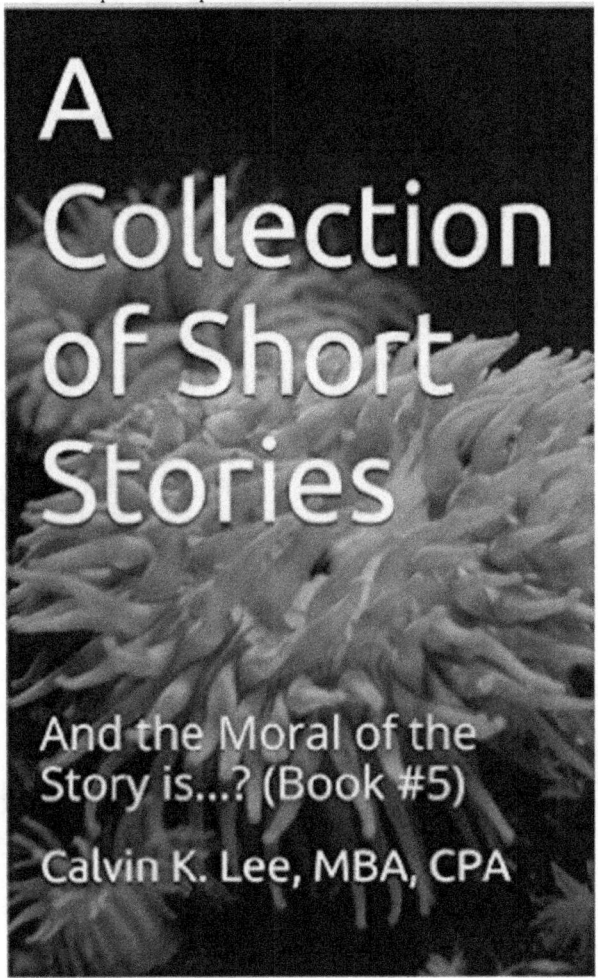

Table of Contents

About the Author
To the reader
The flag and pole (adapted from the blockbuster movie Captain America)
The red and blue crayons
The train
Five planks of wood: unity is power
The magical watches
A school of fish
The well
The animal trap and a benevolent man
Contact the author and final words
Other books by Calvin K. Lee

The flag and pole (adapted from the blockbuster movie *Captain America*)

You can find a video clip of this on Youtube by searching "Captain America pole scene".

A drill sergeant told his unit of soldiers that they were going to have a test. The test will test their physical strength and decision-making ability.

First, the sergeant made the soldiers do pushups. Then they had to crawl through mud. After that they had to run miles throughout the training fields.

Finally, they arrived at their final test. The drill sergeant stood next to tall pole and shouted, "Listen up, soldiers! There's a flag attached to the top of this pole. The first person to get it and bring me the flag passes the test. The rest will have to do pushups, crawl through the mud, and run miles again."

The men jumped on the pole one by one and tried to climb up the pole to get the flag. However, the sergeant in advance had coated the pole with oil so it was really slippery and the soldiers couldn't get a solid grip to climb. They kept sliding back down, often landing on top of each other. "Nobody's gotten that flag in 17 years!" shouted the drill sergeant. After many failed attempts, the soldiers were exhausted and was considering giving up, that the task was impossible.

At this time one of the soldiers, Rogers, walked up to the pole and said he will get the flag. The other soldiers, who were bigger and stronger than Rogers, laughed. They called him "Skinny Rogers" because of his lack of physical strength and skinny frame.

Rogers walked up to the pole, and calmly pulled out the metal piece out of the ground that held the pole vertical. The pole fell to the ground with a thud like a tree being cut down, leaving the flag that was on top of the pole on the ground.

"Hey, that's cheating!" said the other soldiers.

Rogers calmly said, "The sergeant just told to get the flag and bring it to him. He never said taking the pole down was against the rules." Rogers then looked at the sergeant.

"He is correct!" said the sergeant with a smile. "This is not only a test of physical strength, but a test of your decision-making skills and ability to carefully pay attention to instructions! Now all of you, with the exception of Rogers, do your push ups, crawl through the mud, and run miles again!"
Click here to get your copy from Amazon: 5. A Collection of Short Stories: And the Moral of the Story is...? (Book #5)

FREE book sample from:

"Bookkeeping and Accounting Step-by-step Basics for Small & Medium sized Businesses and Home Businesses: Over 20 Examples of Common Accounting Transactions!"
©2015 Calvin Lee
All rights reserved

BOOKKEEPING AND ACCOUNTING STEP-BY-STEP BASICS FOR SMALL & MEDIUM SIZED BUSINESSES AND HOME BUSINESSES

CALVIN K. LEE, MBA, CPA

Over 20 examples of common accounting transactions! (Book #6)

Praise for *"Bookkeeping and Accounting Step-by-step Basics for Small & Medium Sized Businesses and Home Businesses"*

"This is awesome! I love the short chapters with clear examples."

"I'm 100% certain to say that this book should be accounting 100 pre-requisite course for anyone who wants to take introduction to accounting! Very clear, concise, and concrete. Well done!"
- K.T., CPA, CA

Praise from readers of Calvin's books:

"Very practical, good reading!"

"I really enjoy your books."

"Well done, very informative. I like how you used your example."

"By using his own example, Calvin gives hope for the readers."

"Great real life experience that you can relate to easily."

"Very clear, concise, and concrete. Well done."

"Practical tips and relatable examples. A pleasant read. Congratulations on your recent publications! Keep writing more."

"I've taken notes on my smart phone and will implement them in my life."

"Thanks for the little pearls of wisdom and optimism."

Table of Contents

Introduction
Your first day on the job as a bookkeeper or accountant
Types of accounts in accounting
Balance sheet and income statement
Debits and credits must equal
Assets
Liabilities
Revenue
Expenses
Taxes
Accounts receivable
Accounts payable
Purchasing inventory
Inventory costing methods
Lower of cost or market (LCM)
Capital assets
Depreciation of capital assets
Sale of an asset
Shareholder loans – shareholder pays out of pocket
Shareholder loans – company pays on behalf of shareholder
Year-end closing
About the author
Note to the reader
Contact the author
Other books by Calvin K. Lee

Introduction

After reading this book, you will be able to do basic bookkeeping with confidence.

Accounting is the language of business. Whether the company is a global Fortune 500 company or a local mom and pop shop, both of these companies need a system to keep track of income, expenses, assets purchased like computers or furniture, liabilities obtained like mortgages, and equity components such as number of shares issued or how much the owner has invested in the company. Of course, the bigger the company and the more transactions it has, the more complex the accounting.

Small & medium sized businesses and home businesses do not need sophisticated accounting software. They just need a simple system to keep track of the company's transactions. This book is written for beginners to accounting and bookkeeping.

I am a designated CPA accountant in both Canada and the U.S., and have worked since 2007 as an accountant and auditor in public accounting firms and companies. The majority of my clients were small to medium sized businesses. Some of my clients' bookkeepers struggle with the accounting software and the basic accounting concepts.

I have also taught accounting courses at York University's reputable Schulich School of Business in Toronto while I was obtaining a MBA degree myself there. I taught in the Bachelor of Business Administration (BBA) program and Master of Accounting (MAcc) program.

I enjoyed teaching accounting concepts to first year students, and I understand that many of them struggle to learn the accounting language. Textbooks are sometimes long and difficult to follow. My greatest satisfaction in teaching is to explain a concept that is challenging a student, and watch a proverbial light bulb light up as they begin to understand the concept.

Since you've picked up this book, I believe you want to learn the basic concepts of accounting and bookkeeping for small & medium sized enterprises and home businesses. ***I will use the simplest language to explain basic concepts so that you can perform accounting and bookkeeping duties for your business or company.***

This book is designed to be as practical as possible, so I'm going to focus on application rather than explaining detailed theory and concepts.

Think of this book as a quick reference guide rather than a detailed textbook. Therefore, it does not cover all the topics in a first year accounting course. This book covers the most common transactions an entry accountant or bookkeeper will do on a daily basis.

Click here now to get your copy from Amazon: 6. Bookkeeping and Accounting Step-by-step Basics for Small & Medium Sized Businesses and Home Businesses: Over 20 Examples of Common Accounting Transactions! (Book #6)

FREE book sample from:

"Understanding Financial Statement Analysis

for Accountants, Business Owners, Investors, and Stakeholders"

Calvin K. Lee, MBA, CPA, CA, CPA (Illinois)

Understanding Financial Statement Analysis

For Accountants, Business Owners, Investors, and Stakeholders

Calvin K. Lee, MBA, CPA, CA

Table of Contents
1. What you'll get out of this book
2. Balance Sheet - things to watch for
3. Parts of the balance sheet
4. Is lots of cash always a good thing? Not always.
5. Accounts receivable and sales are going up. Great? Maybe not.
6. Inventory - beware of obsolescence
7. Current assets - your first line of defense in business liquidity
8. Current ratio: can this company survive 1 year?
9. Long-term assets - needed to generate future income
10. Property, plant and equipment (PP&E) - watch how they depreciate
11. Intangible assets - essential for some businesses
12. Goodwill - test for impairment
13. Total assets - read the notes and make sure they are all there
14. Return on Assets - did the company make money?
15. Asset turnover ratio - how much revenue did the company make?
16. Current liabilities - pay or face consequences
17. Accounts payable - keep your cash. Delaying payment is good
18. Income taxes payable - do this legally to avoid going to jail
19. Customers' deposits / deferred revenue - not your money...yet!
20. Debts - are they bad or good? It depends
21. Short-term loans - necessary at crucial times
22. Long-term liabilities - a way to fund the business
23. Debt-to-equity ratio - screw this up at your own risk
24. Shareholder's equity - who owns the company?
25. Return on equity - getting your investment money's worth
26. Income statement
27. Revenue - first thing most people look at
28. Cost of sales - let's keep this low
29. Gross margin / gross profit - did we make a profit?
30. Cash flows - cash is king
Final thoughts
Bonus video on balance sheet concepts
About the Author
Note to the reader
Contact the author
Other books by Calvin K. Lee

1. What you'll get out of this book

After reading this book you should have a good understanding of financial statements and reports.

Accounting is the basic language of business. Whether you are an accountant/bookkeeper, a business owner, or an investor, you look at financial statements and reports to determine how well a company is performing.

As a CPA, I look at financial statements every day. I also prepare financial statements for clients. I will share with you in simple terms how to understand and make use of financial statements to achieve your goals.

Where do you start?

Financial statements have several components, including the balance sheet, income statement, cash flow statement, statement of equity, and notes to financial statements.

In my job as a public accountant/auditor I've worked with many different companies. On many days I work with new clients. I have to familiarize myself with the company before doing my audit work.

I start by looking at the notes to the financial statements, usually attached at the end of the financial statements. The notes generally give a good overview of what the company does and introduces the many features in the balance sheet and income statement.

If you're an accountant or bookkeeper who's looking to not only understand financial statements, but also understand the bookkeeping/accounting principles, I suggest you read this book and also my book "Bookkeeping and Accounting Step-by-step Basics for Small & Medium Sized Businesses and Home Businesses: Over 20 Examples of Common Accounting Transactions!" (click here to get a copy in Amazon). In that book I show you the basics of how to do bookkeeping.

Bonus video on balance sheet to further explain concepts at the end of this book! Click here to go to end of book now. There will be a link back here.

2. Balance Sheet - things to watch for

The balance sheet is a historical statement. It is a snapshot at a particular time, usually the year-end of the company.

The balance sheet is usually prepared in the time right after the year-end, usually due for filing with the government 2 or 3 months after the year-end.

Example.
Let's say a company has a year-end of December 31. If you are an investor you are entitled to a copy of the financial statements. Let's say you're an investor looking to invest in a company. You get the financial statements in March of the next year.

You have to remember that the financial statements show the financial performance of a company as at December 31. What has happened in the few months after is not reflected on the financial statements.

If there was a lawsuit that happened subsequent to the date of the financial statements, it would not show on the balance sheet. If the company was sold subsequent to the financial statements date, it would not show on the balance sheet. If new technology was introduced subsequent to the financial statements date, it would not show on the balance sheet.

How to account for these subsequent events?

There are several ways. On the notes to the financial statements, there is a section where management may disclose some foreseeable subsequent events. Another way is to try to get interim financial statements for the new fiscal year subsequent to the year-end financial statements.

URL letter: w

3. Parts of the balance sheet

The balance sheet is generally divided into three main parts. They are:
- Assets
- Liabilities
- Equity

Assets represent the tangible and intangible assets of a company. Tangible assets are things like cash and inventory. Intangible assets include things like goodwill, which is formed when a company purchases another company at a price higher than the net assets of the company being acquired.

Why would a company pay a price higher than the net assets?

It's because the company being acquired has a brand or existing customer list that is worth something and valuable to the company that is acquiring, but these items are not listed on the balance sheet of the company being acquired.

URL letter: a

4. Is lots of cash always a good thing? Not always.

The first asset that is listed is usually cash. Many users of the financial statements, such as accountants/bookkeepers, business owners, investors, creditors, and other stakeholders, look at the amount of cash on hand.

A large cash balance is always good, right?

Wrong. Having a lot of cash on the balance sheet may indicate poor management. Let me explain.

Example.
Cash is sometimes listed as "cash and cash equivalents", meaning any short term liquid investments like certificate of deposits of 30 days are included as "cash". Idle cash doesn't help the company grow its asset base. Perhaps it is better if management puts excess idle cash into investments. I've seen this with some companies. They have lots of cash just sitting there when they should invest it in investments or do something else to make use of their excess cash.

Conclusion:
Unless there is a good reason for the cash balance to be large, such as expecting to pay a large bill or make a purchase, a large cash balance could indicate poor management.

URL letter: t

5. Accounts receivable and sales are going up. Great? Maybe not.

A business usually receives payment from customers in several different forms, including cash or on credit, or a combination of the two.

Accounts receivable is a customer promising to pay in the future in exchange for goods or services now. When a business or company starts up, initially it may grant lenient credit policies to attract more customers.

When customers with lower credit rating are allowed to purchase goods or services on credit, there will usually be more sales. The sales on the income statement increases, and so does accounts receivable. Everything is fine, and business is booming, right?

Maybe.

Example.
A large accounts receivable is useless to a company if they cannot collect cash from customers who promise to pay later. Remember cash is king. If a company doesn't receive cash from its customers, it doesn't matter how many millions of dollars of sales it is generating.

A company must still pay its bills and creditors regardless whether it is collecting cash from its customers or not. Some companies in an attempt to grow sales have done exactly what was described above. But when the company's cash reserves run out, creditors will call loans, and the company may need to fold even though it is generating a lot of sales.

Conclusion:
To put it simply, a large accounts receivable can be a good thing, or it can be a warning sign.

As long as a company can keep collecting cash from its customers listed on the accounts receivable, then it is not in immediate danger. If customers are taking more than 90 days to pay, then the company may have some collection issues.

URL letter: c

Click here to download this book now from Amazon

Calvin K. Lee, MBA, CPA

LEAP before you THINK

Most of us live pretty ordinary lives. Every day we go to work, get off from work, and look forward to the weekend. Every day is so predictable it becomes dreadful, monotonous, boring. We do things on autopilot, and our minds are off wandering elsewhere.

Opportunities come, and opportunities go. Let's pretend the perfect opportunity suddenly showed up in front of you right now, and you have 30 seconds to make up your mind. What would you do?

Most people would panic, because it was not part of the plan. People hesitate, become scared, become reluctant, start asking "what if", and repeat the cycle in their head until they've talked themselves out of it.

Why don't 97% of us live exciting, extraordinary lives? What's holding us back?

FEAR.

Fear holds most of us back. What do we fear? Fear of the unknown. Fear of failure. Fear of rejection. Fear of success. Fear of what others think of us. Fear that we won't know what to do, what to say. Fear that we embarrass ourselves. Fear of ridicule.

What's your fear?

Fear is like a bubble surrounding us. It serves to protects us, but it also prevents 97% of us from realizing our dreams, our potential, our goals, and our destiny.

The good news is, if you can conquer the fear in your life, you gain unlimited power and potential to gain wealth, health, happiness, success, and freedom.

How did fear come into our lives? Most new born children are fearless. They're not afraid of heights as they climbed up the kitchen cabinet to reach for that cookie jar. They're not afraid of saying stupid things. They're not worried about what others think of them when they cry. Children are fearless. They will try anything anywhere, anytime.

But somewhere along the way as we grew up we inherited our fears from other people. We are told that highways are dangerous. We are told that people around us are out to take advantage of us. We are told that we shouldn't dream stupid dreams and become stable and get a steady job. We are taught in school that making a mistake means we are a failure and should feel bad.

Most of us live in a prison in our mind. We are a prisoner of what others think of us. We are so worried about what others think that we dress, act, think, and speak in a way that is socially acceptable. We conform. We lose our uniqueness. We lose ourselves.

The result? We try to blend in. We want to be part of the crowd. We don't want to take risks. We stay in our comfort zone.

Yet deep inside, each of us have a fire inside of us. We have our passions that have been tucked away for so long. That passion may be to learn a new instrument, live in a foreign country, attend graduate school, run for president of the charity we volunteer at, or quit your job and start a business.

We wish...we wish...

And it never happens if we stay wishing. Never. Nada.

LEAP BEFORE YOU THINK

In order to actually feel alive, we must do something. Do anything. It's okay to take baby steps as long as you're moving.

Once you have an idea of what you want to do, you must start to do it. Too many people stop after they dream. They start thinking about the 1,000,000 reasons why they will fail. The longer they think, the more reasons they come up with.

Sometimes the remedy for this paralysis by analysis is to LEAP before you THINK. If you really want to become president of that charity you volunteer at, LEAP before you THINK. Even if you're not sure if you have all the qualifications, raise your hand and volunteer. Believe you can do it.

If you enjoyed this sample, click here to get the full book on Amazon.

About the Author

Calvin K. Lee, MBA, CPA, CA, CPA (Illinois) is an accountant, author, composer, and teacher. He has lived in Beijing, Hong Kong, Toronto, and Vancouver, and travelled to many countries including the U.S.; to Europe such as the U.K., France, Italy, Germany, and Switzerland; and to Asia such as China, Malaysia, Singapore, Japan, and Thailand. Some of his favorite topics include love, relationships, effective communication, psychology, leadership, teamwork, and business. His biggest passion is inspiring and helping others achieve their goals. To do this, Calvin has been writing articles for his blog for over 10 years to inspire and encourage others.

Calvin holds an undergraduate degree from the University of British Columbia in Vancouver, a MBA degree with distinction from York University in Toronto, Canada and is expecting a Double MBA degree from Peking University in Beijing, China in 2016. He is a CPA designated accountant in the U.S. and Canada, and also a Chartered Accountant in Canada. In addition to his successful career in accounting, he has also taught Master of Accounting classes at university, taught accounting modules at the CPA professional association, and enjoys being a mentor to younger accountants. He has served as President of the MBA Ambassadors during his MBA studies and as Chair of the Young Professionals Forum at the CPA Association.

Contact the author

Want a FREE PDF version of this book? Subscribe to my e-mail list by sending an e-mail with the title as the subject line I will e-mail you a free PDF version of this book.

Facebook page: https://www.facebook.com/hellocalvinlee

E-mail: hellocalvinlee@gmail.com
Twitter: @calvinklee2010

If there are any topics you want me to write about in a future book, I'd love to know!
I welcome feedback and comments.

Other books by Calvin K. Lee

Click here to go to my Amazon author page with all my books. *Or click each link below for each book.*

1. How to Increase Confidence and Succeed in Meeting People: Business Networking the Easy Way: Meet New People Now!

2. Living an Extraordinary and Amazingly Purposeful Life: 9 Principles to a Better Life

3. Words of Wisdom, Encouragement, and Inspiration: Bring Happiness into Your Life

4. How to Work Smarter, Not Harder: Success in the Workplace

5. A Collection of Short Stories: And the Moral of the Story is...?

6. Bookkeeping and Accounting Step-by-step Basics for Small & Medium Sized Businesses and Home Businesses: Over 20 Examples of Common Accounting Transactions!

7. Understanding Financial Statements: For Accountants, Business Owners, Investors, and Stakeholders

8. LEAP before you THINK

www.ingramcontent.com/pod-product-compliance
Lightning Source LLC
Chambersburg PA
CBHW071630170526
45166CB00003B/1275